Never Stress You're Definitely Blessed

Katrina Wills Hodges, M.S. C. J.

DEDICATION

Avary,

When God sent you, he sent an Amazing blessing. Always focus on being the brightest shining star in the sky and the pot of gold at the end of the rainbow. Sing when you want to sing, dance, when you feel like dancing, and always smile the biggest smile that can be seen from miles away. Stay confident and know you are not only loved by me but most importantly but God. When things get hard always remember: Never Stress You're Definitely Blessed!!

Love,
GiGi

My Name is Avary!
I am Smart.
I am Special.

We are all different and unique, and yet we are all special because God made each of us in His image.

GENESIS 1:27
God created you and me in His image and likeness. We are special to God.

I am Thankful for
MY FRIENDS

1 Chronicles 16:34

My friends share with me!
Always remember Sharing is Caring

Proverbs 18:24

If you want to have friends be friendly. God will give you friends that will stick beside you.

I LOVE

GOING ON TRIPS

AND HAVING FUN

Trust in the Lord and do good and He will give you your Heart's desire too.
Romans 37:3-4

I AM CONFIDENTLY

ME

I am all that and you are too! Our Confidence is in God!

PROVERBS 3:26

I Love Church And I love to Sing

MY FAVORITE

SONG IS

SUNDAY BEST

God loves me. And I love Him!
His love has set me free and His love can
set you free too!

Psalm 91:1, 4, 14-16

When I Step into a Room my smile always Brighten up Everyone's Day

You can live and be happy too!
You are God's Child! Make the Lord your greatest joy.
Proverbs 10:28

I am God's Chosen one and
he has chosen you to do
great things!

Deuteronomy 7:6

I AM
SPECIAL

AND SO ARE YOU!

Thank you for reading about ME! Always remember that God loves you and so do I...
Avary

Write about what makes you Happy!

Use the following pages to write your own story about what makes you special?

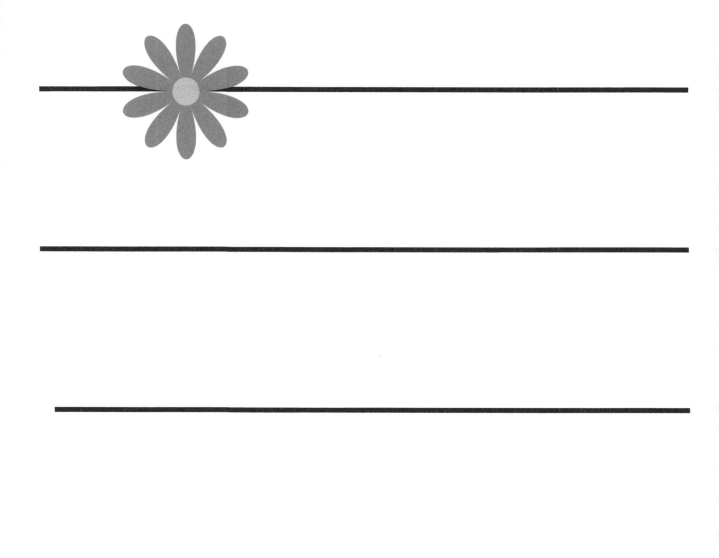

Use the following pages to write your own story about where you would like to travel to?

Use the following pages to write your own story about who your friends are and what do you all like to do when you're together?

On the Following pages write about what kinds of music do you like to listen to? What is your favorite song?

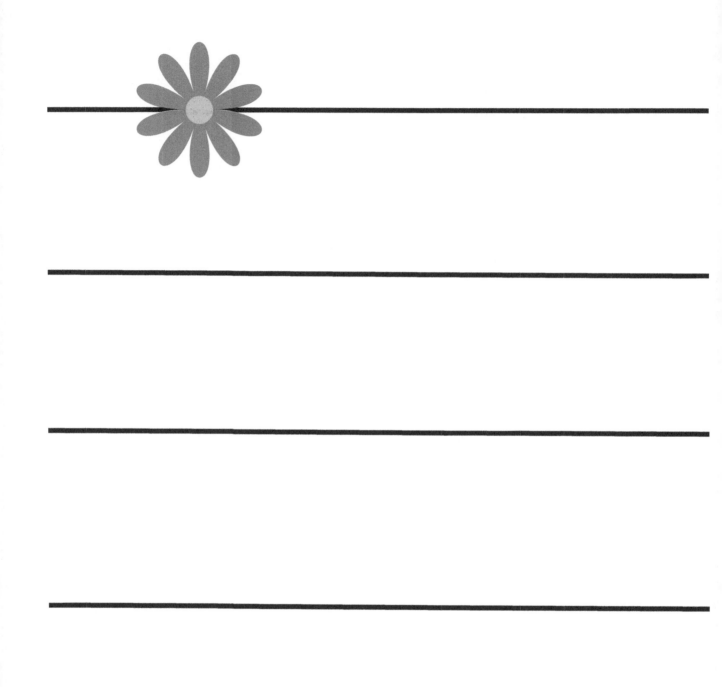

I praise you, for I am fearfully and wonderfully made!
Psalm 139:14

Made in the USA
Coppell, TX
10 May 2022

77585885R00044